Sandhurst Occasional Papers

No 22

CW00541951

Leadership Models and Values: the Agile Officer in a Globalising World

by

Alexander Gardner-McTaggart

Central Library

Royal Military Academy Sandhurst

2017

Introduction

Military Leadership operates in a distinct field, characterised by discipline and conflict, but also by compassion and creativity. 'Command and Control' approaches may be said to accommodate the former, whilst the latter may orient more towards models of 'empowerment'. Such a black and white view of leadership, however, is misleading, as witnessed by the situated phenomenon of German *Auftragstaktik*. For a military force entering into the diverse globalised arena of the 21st century an understanding of the most pertinent leadership approaches is likely to be beneficial. For an army aiming to train an agile officer, quick thinking based upon theory and values appears to be key.

Leadership begins in the individual. Leading oneself is vital in being able to engage in the social world, to influence and orient others to a particular cause or objective. In this process, team leadership is essential in tackling the new challenges thrown up by the eclectic nature of a rapidly globalising world. Habermas (1987) warns of the insidious creep of 'technicism' in the Neo Liberal globalising world. This is where society is altered due to technology, and the human element is obviated in a problem-fix solution culture. It is the march of positivism at a global level, where, driven by market forces, numbers and figures produce solutions to global issues. This sentiment was echoed by Prince Charles (Gye, 2015) in last year's passing out parade at Sandhurst, praising the British understanding of the human factor, and stressing the importance of empathy in the face of technology. These challenges are well addressed in pedagogy through the process of social constructivism, as outlined by Lev Vygotsky (1978). It is one where the individual attains identity and character though a process mediated between self, and the

1

group. This on-going dialectic is one that builds connection to abstract ideas and models, establishing emotional connection to rational concepts, and developing values in the affective domain. In this way, the identity of leadership (based on values) can only materialise in team interaction, with empathy, guided by conceptual rigour. As a result, and as this paper will argue, the development of team leadership and the development of values profit enormously when developed in a symbiotic relationship.

Leadership Models

Leadership can be difficult to define, yet what is clear is that leadership and management are distinct, and offer two quite different aspects of 'running' an organisation or group. A quotation from an inspirational website catches the idea behind management and leadership. 'Management is doing things right, leadership is doing the right things.' (Drucker, 2001). It is clear that the roles of leadership and management often blur; a leader still needs to address organisation, and a manager still needs to make decisions. However, in unpicking this sentence it emerges that the role of management may be perceived as a following of rules and implementing policy, whereas the role of leadership is bound to an ethical and moral orientation, vision, and direction. In this way, leadership finds apposite recognition in this quotation: 'The supreme quality for a leader is unquestionably integrity. Without it, no real success is possible, no matter whether it is on a section gang, a football field, in an army or in an office.' Dwight D. Eisenhower in Kiisel (2013, p. 1). Bear in mind that this is the quotation of a soldier, and the emphasis is on 'Moral' leadership. Yet, this still falls in line with an approach that seeks to keep the human element intact: a vital component of leadership in a technicist age (Habermas, 1987). Despite the overlap between roles, models of leadership and management are considered separately, for example in figure 1.1 with Bush and Glover:

Management Model	Leadership Model
Formal	Managerial
Collegial	Participative, Transformational, Distributed
Political	Transactional
Subjective	Postmodern, Emotional
Ambiguity	Contingency
Cultural	Moral

Fig. 1.1 (Bush, 2011, p. 36)

The leadership models this paper deals with fall in to the Managerial, Participative, Transformational, Distributed, Transactional, Contingency and Moral.

Officer Leadership Orientation

The RMA Sandhurst's use of Adair's Action Centred Leadership (ACL) (Adair, 1968) has recently been added to by 'transformational theory', and most recently the British army has taken up a 'Values Based' leadership model (Vincent, 2015). With the introduction of the publication *Developing leaders: a British Army Guide*, (Ministry of Defence, 2014) Vincent contends that this new orientation encompasses a combination of UK Values Based Leadership and the US Army's Be, Know, Do framework (Vincent, 2015, p. 5). In the following section, this paper addresses the leadership orientation through the lens of leadership models.

Adair

Adair's ACL is leader-led. This is clear as its emphasis on developing the team and developing the individual (supporting, agreeing, recognising, enabling facilitating) (Adair, 1968; Adair, 2003), whilst the function of the leader remains to initiate and manage these processes. In this way, ACL could be argued in terms of management as a *formal model*, or in leadership as a *managerial model*.

> In a managerial model it is assumed that outside influences are transmitted through [leaders] whose knowledge of the external environment reinforces their official authority. The leaders' interpretation of these pressures may then be a significant element in the decision making process.
>
> (Bush, 2011, pp. 115-116).

However, with the influence (support, agreement, recognition) that is granted groups and individuals in a leader-led process it appears that ACL falls more succinctly in line with a *political* model of management, and a *transactional* model of leadership. 'In political models it is thought that external factors may be introduced by interest groups as well as by [leaders].' In this way, it is understood that subordinates may cite their own valid external evidence, gaining recognition and involvement. However, this is not without added burden on the leader, as '... these environmental pressures mingle with the internal factors and add to the complexity and ambiguity of decision making (Bush, 2011, p. 116). Transactional leadership is said to be characterised by three dimensions:

- *Contingent reward.* The degree to which the leader sets up constructive exchanges with followers.
- *Management by exception – active.* Active leaders monitor follower behaviour, anticipate problems, and take corrective actions.
- *Management by exception – passive.* Passive leaders wait until the behaviour has caused problems before taking action.

  (Judge & Piccolo, 2004, p. 755).

When viewed in this way, transactional leadership appears to accommodate ACL comfortably within its framework.

Values

On the other hand, 'values based leadership' addresses more significantly organisational culture and can be equated with a model of moral leadership.

> The leadership model most closely linked to organisational culture is that of *moral leadership.* This model assumes that the critical focus of leadership ought to be on the values, beliefs and ethics of leaders themselves. Authority and influence are to be derived from defensible conceptions of what is right or good. (Leithwood et al., 1999:10). These authors add that this model includes normative, political/democratic and symbolic aspects of leadership.
> (Bush, 2011, p. 184)

This focus on values, beliefs and ethics of leaders themselves, is reminiscent of Eisenhower's idea of leadership as cited above. It is an officer and soldier expressive of the subjective experience as a lived phenomenon, leaving a call for rich phenomenological research in this area. Indeed, a conceptualisation of officer leadership is then bound (at the subject) to moral leadership. This view is also confirmed by Vincent's non-academic SMEs (Vincent, 2015) who focus on values for leadership. However, Bush (above) acknowledges that a moral leadership certainly *includes* normative and other aspects of leadership. As a result, the British Army's identification of transformational leadership (normative aspect) is not an uncommon companion of moral leadership, but it is unclear how this normative aspect embodies in leadership, or indeed what effects it may produce in this distinct military field. This suggests an area for further research.

Normative versus Descriptive

Normative aspects of leadership tend to be theories. They are a reflection of beliefs of how leading should occur. Indeed, when theorists express how a leadership process should be managed, e.g., transformational or transactional, they are expressing normative judgements, rather than analysing actual practice (Bush, 2011, p. 29). The need for research here is clear in order for theory to be used descriptively. Vincent provides a useful description use of theory, and further on I shall engage with my own research results in order to posit comparative descriptive data.

The Agile Officer and Globalisation

Vincent (2015) has identified the 'agile officer' as the future of the British army officer leadership: and this viewpoint is echoed in

'Developing Leaders'. A review of some literature shows that there are varying viewpoints on how to address this normative stance on leadership.

In recent mixed methods research it emerges that there is some contention surrounding the issue of values based leadership, with Subject Matter Expert *(SME)* groups taking different stances (Vincent 2015). This variance can be broadly understood as a difference between academic and military conceptualisations of leadership. Understandably, scholarly leadership SME's preferred a more informed approach to leadership, with an understanding of established theory of leadership models: in its diversity. Conversely, military SMEs were compelled by values: i.e. a moral model of leadership.

It is clear that the world today faces different challenges and opportunities, and mostly this is associated with the increasing reach of markets in a globalising age. This time is characterised by an 'annihilation of distance', one that is 'dissociative and alienating' (Heidegger, 1971, p. 164). With technology the fuel of globalisation, this runs parallel to Habermas (1987) and the technicist agenda, reaffirming the need for 'the human touch' as outlined by Prince Charles at the 179th Sovereign's parade at Sandhurst 2015.

In the face of globalisation, fuelled by markets, opportunities and threats change rapidly, and the affordance of modern technology facilitates this change (Held & McGrew, 2007). The call for an adaptive and 'agile' officer is a timely reaction to the global status quo. In approaching leadership for this globalised age, it is important to consider models that are not merely in sync with change, but that are born of it.

In the following section, this paper will reflect upon leadership models, with a contrast of 'command and control' models, and 'empowerment' models, with an eye to explore how independence and initiative can work to the benefit of the officer, amidst globalising change.

Command and Control

Traditional military leadership models focusing on Command and Control are identified as being a top-down and intentionally conservative system, as outlined below:

> You can recognise command and control by its hierarchical and top down reporting structure. Command and control organisations and leadership rely on control as the organising force. This means that tools such as the budget, strategic plan, and compensation program are used in ways that control the actions and outcomes of people and processes to meet stated plan and objectives. When used in a command and control environment, these tools are designed to control, predict and limit specific behaviours and outcomes. The overall goal is to design out as many variables as possible in order to minimise external and internal disruptions to the organisations plans and strategies. In a command and control environment change is generally viewed as an unwelcome disruption to the status quo because it brings instability, newness, creativity and

unpredictability-all things that threaten the existing
stability of the system.

(Olson & Singer, 2004, p. 2)

Whilst controlling, predicting and taking out variables may have its appeal, the above quotation makes clear how this model is not designed for rapid change and unpredictability. This system of leadership may present a normative outlook for battlefield scenario where focus is on maintaining control and overview, and running counter to traditions such as the Wehrmacht's *Auftragstaktik*. The world is changing, and as outlined in Vincent (2015), Command and Control is clearly not a leadership model that will address the MoD's need to innovate, seize and hold initiative and make quick decisions having identified the risks. Nor will it best serve the 'agile officer' to be able to deal with ambiguity and uncertainty, as pointed out by Forrest, Leggatt, and Kelly (2012). Instead, command and control fits into what has previously been termed a *formal* form of management, which translates as a *managerial* form of leadership (Bush, 2011, p. 36). Here Bush: 'Formal models assume that organisations are hierarchical systems in which managers use rational means to pursue agreed goals.' (Bush, 2011, p. 40). This could also be a place for the Authoritarian/Coercive forms of Leadership as dealt with by Walsh (2014, pp. 14-15).

These are valued for their ability to deliver results and be highly effective. However, Walsh is also quick to point out (as is Bush with managerial models) that such leadership is often characterised by the micro-manager and a stifling of initiative from subordinates. Such leadership is best surmised thus: 'It [Authoritarian Leadership] is a seductive habit, but a dangerous one, for any organisation that requires leaders to face up to situations marked by their uncertainty, unpredictability and complexity (Walsh, 2014, p. 15).

Further aspects of a Command and Control outlook are likely to include Transactional Leadership. This form of leadership is generally considered to belong to the political group based upon power, and the 'reward' or 'punishment' of preferred and dis-preferred behaviours respectively, often said to involve micro politics (Bush, 2011). This model is identified by Maddan (2014) as being central to the British Army leadership ethos. However, Maddan stresses a judicial and balanced implementation of transactional leadership, and in this way describes transactional leadership in line with Adair's ACL, a connection that has already been made in this paper above. Further, Maddan cautions of the erratic and arbitrary implementation of this model, due to its being demotivating and divisive. Maddan deals with transactional leadership at length, summarising thus: 'Leaders who create a climate of trust, motivation and achievement, underpinned by the values and standards of the British Army, can raise the overall output of the organisation and assist in retention.' (p. 28). This appears to echo Adair's stress on the motivating, facilitating, and acknowledging that must occur in ACL, in order for this leader led model to achieve best results (Adair, 1968; Adair, 2003).

All in all, the challenge with these models is that they stress the structural competence of hierarchy over the character of the leader. This may be a valid point for the purported direction of an army that seeks to empower leadership of character, through values. However, times have changed, and with them battlefields. Such a leadership environment may no longer be able to offer fertile ground for agile thinkers and doers, in turbulent times. In formal models, the personality of leadership is subservient to the 'rank'. Indeed, this may appear to be more reminiscent of the Red Army's *Orchestra* metaphor, where every component plays its part, and is compliant with the conductor.

Finally, it is clear that the world is witnessing a change in leadership orientation. Aside from the literature with a British army origin, this paper borrows from various fields of (public) service. The move in leadership is well conceived here in borrowing from the field of policing here in figure 2.1:

Traditional and Contemporary Models of Policing

Traditional	Contemporary
Policing as trade/craft	Policing as profession
Authoritarian approach to policing	Problem solving
Quasi military management style	Democratic management style
Emphasis on physical attributes	Emphasis on intelligence
Insular and defensive culture	Open and consultive culture

Fig. 2.1. Murray 2002 in Mitchell & Casey (2007, p. 149)

As is clear, the leadership models currently in vogue follow a general trend, which is at once decentralised, collaborative, and involving. This paper now turns to these 'empowering' models of leadership.

Empowerment Models

In contrast to a Command and Control model of leadership, 'empowerment models': are geared for innovation and change. Termed *collegial* in management, these are typically *participative, transformational* and *distributed* as leadership models. They aim to empower the leader with involved subordinates, and shy from the autocratic 'top down' approach to leadership, enabling individual agency (Bush, 2007) motivating team-members intrinsically rather than extrinsically. Leaders become enablers, who mentor responsibility and leadership in others, allowing team members to feel some element of ownership in their work, pride in what they do, and responsibility for their actions. With team members invested in the process, the organisation is thought to become more empowered. The advantage in this approach over a formal structural method is that individual agency is tapped, and team potential strengthened rather than stifled. As the 'collegial' management label attests, this is a model geared for teamwork. This does not mean that the leader becomes less potent; it simply means that leadership becomes a team affair. The leader commands empowered players, rather than 'pawns'.

Empowerment models sound 'great'. However, a closer reading of these models makes it clear how much more challenging this leadership style may be, due to its interpersonal complexity. In these forms, leadership requires a great deal of knowledge of 'how to lead' (and an understanding of leadership models), and with it, developed physical skills, coupled with emotional intelligence.

Distributed, Participative, and Transformative models (Bush, 2011) are most common among the empowerment models. Walsh (2014) discusses Participative leadership in the military context as one of four 'path-goal' models, and in this context, it is often conceived of as a sharing of pertinent information, engendering a recognition and value of the subordinate and their own intelligence. The example of participative leadership is given via Field Marshalls Montgomery and Slim, and via Marshall Rokossovskiy. The distribution of contextual (battlefield) knowledge and involvement of subordinates is best summed up by the latter thus '... believe an old soldier: there is nothing a man prizes more than the realisation that he is trusted, believed relied upon.' (Rokosovskiy, 2002, p. 122).

Moral, transformational and transactional

Maddan (2014, p. 20) points out how 'Values based leadership' *(VBL)* is the application of an appropriate mix of inspirational and transactional leadership behaviours underpinned by the values and standards of the British Army.' In unpacking this statement it emerges that there is indeed a clear idea of how leadership manifests. He sees VBL evident in the *Developing leaders: a British Army Guide* (Ministry of Defence, 2014), cites transformational leadership as a recent addition to officer leadership (Ministry of Defence, 2004).

> For 50 years RMAS has used John Adair's (1968)
> Action Centred Leadership added to in the last 10 years
> by Transformational Theory (MOD, 2004). However,
> since 2008 the British Army has expounded a model of
> Values Based Leadership (MOD, 2008), which is now

the method of teaching and evaluating leadership at
RMAS.

(Vincent, 2015, p. 4)

In articulating these approaches to leadership as models, it emerges that
the RMA Sandhurst aims to facilitate moral leadership (VBL) with
aspects of transformational leadership (inspirational), and a perceived
aspect of transactional leadership (ACL). In terms of moral and
transformative models, this is confirmed by Maddan who states:
'Academically VBL is underpinned by Transformational Leadership
Theory, however it selectively uses terminology that suits a military
audience.' (Maddan, 2014, p. 20). This raises a contentious point, as the
relationship between transformational and transactional models is often
viewed as highly related, although this view is contested. This is dealt
with in some detail below.

Transformational

Transformational leadership has the advantage of being able to
transition discrete organisational bodies into self-managing units. Here I
borrow from the example of school leadership.

Transformational leaders succeed in gaining the
commitment of followers to such a degree that ... higher
levels of accomplishment become virtually a moral
imperative. In our view a powerful capacity for
transformational leadership is required for the successful
transition to a system of self-managing schools.

(Bush, 2007, p. 396)

Indeed, this researcher's recent study on senior international schools' leadership and globalisation reveals (and confirms) perceived beliefs in Anglo-American leadership practice (Northouse, 2010) on transformational leadership. In line with the International Baccalaureate 'distributed leadership' was cited as the preferred normative model of leadership by five of six participants. However, in critical analysis, it emerged that *distributed,* hid the fact that *transformational* leadership that was indeed most compelling (and most operationalized) to the Anglo-American leaders in the sample. Further it found in four of five cases that transformational went hand in hand with a transactional model.

The transformational leader is not without criticism, perhaps explaining the orientation of leaders in my sample, away from the transformational. Leaders operationalizing this leadership model are said to tend towards a leadership style, which raises 'moral qualms' in a democratic organisation (such as a school) as the leadership style may become 'despotic' (Allix, 2000). Walsh confirms Allix, connecting transformational leadership with the charismatic, and questioning whether '… transformational leadership is just an intellectualisation of the trait theory school that produces dominant, self-appointed leaders who engage in little genuine interaction with followers.' (Walsh, 2014, p. 12). Indeed, empirical data on leadership models extends this theoretical premise, by exposing how transformational leadership does not always fare well, given the pressures of globalisation. The shadow side of this type of leadership in this context lies in a normative (transformational) discourse cloaking an arbitrary and rigid 'transactional' approach to leadership (Gardner-McTaggart, 2017).

Situated leadership

In a globalising world, eclecticism is the order of the day. This is apparent from the perception of *Epoch* or *Era* in Philosophy, Arts and Culture. Eras reflect societal orientation, such as Romanticism, Classism, Modernism, Impressionism, Expressionism, and most recently in the form of Post-Modernism. This zeitgeist of the time is in this way apparent in leadership studies as forms of leadership, which aim to embrace the heterogeneous nature of the world, and act accordingly. The challenges with such an approach lie in the intellectual, as 'knowing' becomes increasingly important, and understanding the many different approaches to leadership is central.

In this researcher's own study, participant director *Alfred* refers to his own leadership model in this way, calling it a 'basket of resources'. In example, the director relates how his approach aims to enable his staff: *everyone is a leader* (distributed leadership). However, in times of crisis, he was forced to become the change agent (transformational leadership), but in order to achieve this, he evinced change not in the typical manner of transformational leadership, but employed an arbitrary system of punishment and reward (transactional leadership). With this process over, he was clear in informing all participants of his motivation, and orientation (participative leadership) (Gardner-McTaggart, 2017). This approach led to much conflict, but Alfred is clear that he got the job done, and mentions how the previous five directors had only survived one year in the post, and he is in his seventh year.

In military terms, the lessons of 'Auftragstaktik' and Israeli 'situational awareness' (Walsh, 2014, p. 8) confirm the conflict inherent in a model of situational leadership. It is a model that reacts to the pressures unfolding in situ, making it difficult to plan for, and placing heavy demands on the leader at the coal face. Walsh makes a strong case for a Situated Leadership approach in pursing leadership for the agile leader. This form of leadership requires intellect, an understanding of theory, and the ability to react quickly with appropriate strategies that fit the demand of the unfolding action.

Leadership Character and Globalisation

The character of leadership has been central to an understanding of what an officer is in the British army, highlighted by Vincent (2015, p. 23) in citing the 1947 British Army officer's guide: '... officers must be the embodiment of leadership, character and the Army Core Values.' Values can be elusive and this is recognised in the Combat Infantryman's Course (CIC2012) where: 'It acknowledges the need for continual values and leadership education in NCOs who receive far less formal leadership training than officers.' (Maddan, 2014, p. 21). However, *leadership, character and values* leave a great deal of room for maneuverer and interpretation, a point which Madden cautions of as '... a risk of personal interpretation of Army values based on personal beliefs.' Unless the very nature of these three elements is explored, analysed and identified in rigorous theoretical setting, with experiential articulation, it is difficult to imagine how this leading sentence can be of substantive help to a young officer in the field.

Leadership character and values in the International Baccalaureate

In the following section I will draw further upon my recent research on educational leadership in the globalising context (Gardner-McTaggart, 2017) in order to illuminate how a values based system of leadership can operate. The aim of this study was to explore the character (not the characteristics) of senior leadership in International Baccalaureate *(IB)* schools in Western Europe through the lens of the IB Learner Profile *(IBLP)*. The values based IB system provides a leadership template in the form of the IBLP. This is a set of ten attributes by which values are conveyed to the student body, the faculty, and indeed, leadership. Research aims included an exploration of how the Leaders operationalized the IBLP in leadership, and how their character influenced this.

Research design

The study was conducted longitudinally over two years with a purposive sample of six participants, all directors of medium to large IB international schools in Switzerland, Austria and Germany. Data collection aimed to get close to the participant, and the researcher was familiar with the research context as a working professional embedded in this schools' context as middle manager and teacher in an international school in a different global region. Data collection was in the form of pre-interview data stimulus, face to face unstructured interview, observation, follow up review of transcripts, follow up review of findings chapters, and subsequent emailed questions as and when needed. Data was coded and divided into basic themes, and then on into organising themes. Organising themes were presented in a cross case analysis. Analysis drew upon critical theory, predominantly in the work of Bourdieu, educational leadership theory, and involved a degree of critical phenomenological interpretation.

Findings

It emerged that leaders faced a tension between their normative educational practice and the rigid reality of the globalised marketplace. This put them at odds with the non-market orientation of educational practice. Herein lies a parallel with the British Army leadership and a rapidly globalising market oriented world. In this study, it emerged that the international educational context, whilst seemingly distinct from market forces, was in fact deeply entwined with the economic profit-seeking logic of commercial enterprise. In drawing parallels, it is to be expected that the British Army is also connected with market factors, much as posited by Carl von Clausewitz's (1832) contention that the process of economics and war were intrinsically linked and similar. Clausewitz appears in this way to address certain truths that may be more relevant now than ever.

In my own research, it was found that values were central to participants' leadership approach. Much as with Clausewitz, this study employed critical analysis, which revealed that the values espoused by participants were without exception, Anglo-European and in the Christian-Hellenic tradition. Whilst thematically similar, these values were all subject to interpretation of the individual in question. This was a significant finding for an international schools' system, conferring the continuing influence and validity of Anglo-Christian thinking in a post-colonial world, but also the vagaries inherent in VBL.

A disadvantage of VBL is the fact that participants can 'choose' where their values lie, according to their needs. A good example of this is drawn from the Analysis chapter where the value of being a *risk taker* is used ambiguously. The study is rich, and here follows an extract from director 'Elvin' and one core IB value; *Risk Taker*:

> Elvin relates a struggle with the board, especially as regards his conception of 'risk taking'. One project of his failed, and the board took a very dim view: an example of how international school boards work. As related in the literature review, they are very often market oriented, transient, not educationally oriented and vary greatly (Bunnell, 2005). Elvin argues that, from a constructivist approach, risk taking implies learning, yet the board were not open to the concept at an operational level and do not tolerate 'mistakes', which Elvin views as 'risk taking'. This is perhaps a very pertinent example of the responsibility put on an IB director to 'translate' the rigid market-driven economics of globalised board parameters into normative educational parlance. Alternatively, it may simply be the board expecting the director to be 'finished with his learning', and not a 'lifelong learner'. This could be construed as a convenient way for Elvin to reinterpret the IBLP according to his needs, (a feature Charles found problematic in using the IBLP with the issue of being 'principled' used by himself and his teachers in different ways: underlining the IBLP paradox of Stevenson et al. (2014)). This would confirm Kaplan and Kaiser's (2003) proposal that an understanding of the dualities of leadership does not give permission to switch sides to avoid conflict. More, it is a call for

integrity and the IBLP and IB mission statement provide the framework for such integrity; it could be precisely the 'unifying ethos' required for leadership in the disparate International schools sector (Matthews & Sidhu, 2005; Hill, 2006). However, in the eyes of the board, this may be simply blaming failure on the IB – switching sides for convenience. Whichever way this is treated, it serves to underscore the tensions apparent in the international IB school.

Gardner-McTaggart (2007), *Analysis*, p. 20

It is clear that a values based approach to leadership is not without challenges, yet what emerges in this International IB study, is that the values are in place, but conformity to these values is not: participant *Dorothy* is the exception that proves the rule.

There are certain significant factors emerging from the above research that appear to affect leadership by values. The *IBLP Handbook* is an organisational guide intended, amongst others, for leadership. In unstructured interview, only one of the six participants (*Dorothy*) mentioned reading and actively using the *IBLP Handbook*. (It is interesting to note - in comparison - that at RMA Sandhurst, 54% of participants had not read the *British Army: Developing Leaders Guide* and Vincent reports a correspondingly weak understanding of team leadership techniques (Vincent, 2015, p. 10)). *Dorothy* was then the only participant who related a clearly structured IBLP approach to leadership, stressing team leadership and utilising the values of the IBLP in every facet of her administration. She also related the values as a tool for establishing common ground, and embedding a shared language of leadership. The end result was a clear and articulated use and on-going conversation surrounding the IB values.

To sum up, the above research in International IB leadership found that values and transformational models of leadership are the preferred model. (Herein lies a parallel to the British Army leadership based upon values and the transformational). Yet, the research also brought to light, how rigid and normative outlooks, whilst seemingly at odds, exist side by side in leadership, confirming the claim that '... transformational and transactional leadership are so highly related that it makes it difficult to separate their unique effects (Judge & Piccolo, 2004, p. 765). This serves as an anaphoric reference to the above discussion on transformational and transactional forms of leadership serving as aspects of VBL in the British Army, above.

Mixed messages in leadership

This research uncovered a uniformity in leadership of globalisation. It is one that needs to appear to be empowering, but in order to survive, tends towards the rigid (formal, transactional). Further to the above point in regard to empowerment models (distributed, participative, transformational), Hartley has argued that this is a situation where the '... discourse of distributed leadership may persist, even if as a practice it does not. It may provide a collegial and democratic veneer to the creeping rational real-time digitisation of the management of education.' (2016, p. 181). Leadership approaches that aim to adapt to the rapid changes of globalisation, face a very real threat of paying lip service to collegial/empowerment models, whilst actually cloaking transformational/transactional realities. In other words, it is compelling to espouse aspects of leadership that are 'fashionable' or desirable. Yet it is more difficult to pull the theoretical into the physical domain.

Teaching Leadership

The agile classroom is where the teaching of leadership must explore the three domains of human activity as presented in *Bloom's Taxonomy* (Bloom, 1984). In such a team environment, leadership grows through a shared negotiation of concepts in practice, and connecting with values that form the character of leadership in the British Army. This is the 'affective domain' - vital in facilitating a 'felt', and 'embodied' articulation of values that reify the character of leadership. Making values clear, collective, and character: '... consistent practice assists in embedding the Army's values into the leaders' own character so that they become inherent.' (Maddan, 2014, p. 22). In this way, any form of leadership training that aspires to affect character with values must invest itself in cognitive and physical group activity, in order to implement affective growth.

- *Cognitive:* theories of leadership, transformational, situational, transactional, values based.
- *Affective:* connection to values, expression of values, collective negotiation of values.
- *Physical:* skills in leadership, charisma, confidence, clarity.

A demanding physical and mental course of 44 weeks such as that at RMAS addresses all three domains, and offers a rich opportunity for the active pedagogue to embrace multisensory and experiential teaching, through collaboration and coordination.

Further Research

Vincent provides helpful recommendations from his mixed methods study. For example: a better definition of values based leadership, reintroduction of Adair's model from which to use Values Based leadership and intensification or discontinuation of the US Army inspired Be, Do, Know framework. Further, a higher emphasis on the conceptual training of 'Be' and, an exploration of ethics in Army leadership, the addition of 'belief' to Be, Know, Do. Indeed, consideration that the British Army's values based leadership may be cognisant with 'Authentic leadership theory', and finally, the very real and valid question of whether, in its current form, the British Army leadership outlook is prepared for the agile age (Vincent, 2015, pp. 29-30). Further research is clearly of value into two main areas: transformative and transactional synergy in moral leadership and the tensions between situated and moral leadership in the agile officer.

Methodological orientation

Previous research in this area appears to have no clear antipositivst foundation. The very unique phenomenon of officer leadership in this present time of globalising change offers up a singular chance for the phenomenologist researcher to shed light on normative assumptions of leadership and move the discussion into the rich descriptive field. The field of army leadership, specifically at RMAS may be in a position to exploit the implementation of interpretivist research, in the critical paradigm. Centrally, any attempt at phenomenological proximity, the opportunity to 'get close' to participants, and engage in understanding the nature of being an officer is compelling. It is clear that such research is time intensive, but the potential for building a unique and excellent descriptive knowledge base on the phenomena of being an officer in Her Majesty's Armed forces is given. A major limiting aspect of such research lies in finding a research approach which protects participants with anonymity. Whilst limiting, the study on directors above faced similar contextual challenges, which were indeed surmountable.

Overview

It appears that the agile officer must be in a position to respond to global threats in a rapidly changing world. Optimum leadership in this eclectic age must therefore draw upon the practicality of empirical experience in the field, informed by the best there is to offer in theory. With the march of technicism, and the dissociative effects of globalisation, soldier officers find strong resonance to what they do in values, character and what can be termed a moral modal of leadership. However, in doing so they must work in teams, and develop empathy and 'the human touch'. Transformational and transactional models of leadership seem to be valued by both academics and officers, and offer ways to articulate from a basis of moral leadership. However, from an informed perspective of theory, a situated form of leadership appears to best accommodate the agility required of officer cadets that may best serve the United Kingdom in a changing world.

Values are key, as is empathy and team leadership, yet these elements must be clearly lived in the affective domain. Leadership models require formal theoretical facilitation, at higher level study. In an agile classroom, the cadet must be able to conceive, feel, and apply their leadership.

Whilst orientations appear here in this paper, questions remain. If future researchers are to understand the phenomenon of leadership as an officer in the British Army, they must do so by combining knowledge as it occurs 'in the field' with theory. The opportunity lies in the anti-positivist paradigm.

Works Cited

Adair, J. (2003). *The Inspirational Leader*. London: Kogan-Page.

Adair, J. (1968). *Training for Leadership*. London: Macdonald.

Allix, N. (2000). Transformational leadership: Democratic or despotic? . *Educational Management and Administration , 28*, 7-20.

Bloom, B. (1984). *Taxonomy of Educational Objectives*. Addison Wesley Publishing Company; 2nd edition edition .

Bunnell, T. (2005). An insight into the board structures of international schools. *International schools journal* .

Bush, T. (2007). Educational leadership and management: theory, policy, and practice . *South African Journal of Education , 27* (3), 391-406.

Bush, T. (2011). *Theories of Educational Leadership and Management fourth edition*. London: Sage.

Drucker, P. (2001). *The essential Drucker*. New York: Harper Collins.

Forrest, E., Leggatt, A., & & Kelly, C. (2012). Understanding What is meant by Individual Agility. *Development Concepts and Doctrine Centre*.

Gardner-McTaggart. (2017). *The International Baccalaureate and Globalisation; implications for educational leadership*. Nottingham: University of Nottingham.

Gye, H. (2015, December 12). *Prince Charles warns Army's newest officers about ISIS 'death cult' they must fight as they pass out from Sandhurst*. Retrieved December 1, 2016, from Mail Online: http://www.dailymail.co.uk/news/article-3356133/Prince-Charles-warns-Army-s-newest-officers-cult-death-destruction.html

Habermas, J. (1987). *The Theory of Communicative Action: Lifeworld and System, a Critique of Functionalist Reason* (Vol. 2). Boston: Beacon Press.

Hartley, D. (2016). Economic crisis, technology and the management of education. *Educational management administartion and leadership , 44* (2).

Heidegger, M. (1971). *Peotry, Langage, Thought*. (A. Hofstadter, Trans.) New York: Harper and Row.

Held, D., & McGrew, A. (2007). *Globalisation Theory*. Cambridge, UK: Polity Press.

Hill, I. (2006). Internationally minded schools. *International Schools Journal , 20* (1), 24-37.

Judge, T., & Piccolo, R. (2004). Transformational and Transactional Leadership: a meta-analytic test of their relative validity. *Journal of Applied Psychology , 89* (5), 755-68.

Kaplan, R., & R, K. (2003). Developing versatile leadership. *MIT Sloan Management Review , 44* (4), 19–26.

Kiisel, T. (2013, February 5). Without it no real success is possible. *Forbes Magazine* .

Klausewitz, C. (1832). *Vom Kriege*. Berlin: Dummers Verlag.

Maddan, D. (2014). Values Based Leadership. *Leadership: Proceedings of a Symposium Held at RMAS*. Camberley: Central Library RMAS.

Matthews, J., & Sidhu, R. (2005). Desperately seeking the global subject: International education, citizenship and cosmopolitanism. . *Globalisation, Societies and Education , 3* (1), 49–66.

Ministry of Defence. (2014, January). Developing Leaders A British Army Guide. *DIRECTOR GENERAL LEADERSHIP* .

Ministry of Defence. (2004). *Leadership in Defence.* Defence Leadership Centre, Shrivenham.

Mitchell, M., & Casey, J. (2007). *Police Leadership and Mangement.* Sydney: The Federation Press.

Northouse, P. (2010). *Leadership Theory and Practice* . London: Sage.

Olson, C., & Singer, P. (2004). Winning with Library Leadership: Enhancing Services Through Connection, Contribution, & Collaboration . In C. Olson, & P. Singer. Chicago: American library association.

Rokosovskiy, K. (2002). *Soldatskiy Dolg.* Olma Press.

Stevenson, H., Thompson, P., & Fox, S. (2014). *IB Middle Years Programme in the UK: Implementation Practices and Student Outcomes Associated with the Learner Profile Attribute 'Open - Minded'.* The University of Nottingham, Faculty of Social Science. The University of Nottingham.

Vincent, D. (2015). B, Know or Do? An analysis of the Optimal Balance of the Be, Know, Do, Leadership Framework in the Future Training at the Royal Military Academy Sandhurst. *Sandhurst Occasional Papers No. 20* .

Vygotsky, L. (1978). *Mind in Society: the development of higher psychological processes.* Harvard University Press.

Walsh, S. (2014). A historical Overview of Leadership. *Leadership: Proceedings of a Symposium eld at the Royal Military Academy Sandhurst, April, 2014* (pp. 1-19). Camberley: Central Library RMAS.

Sandhurst Occasional Papers Series

This series is available online at:
http://www.army.mod.uk/training_education/24565.aspx